# VENTRILOQUISM IN A NUTSHELL

from

MAHER VENTRILOQUIST STUDIOS

Compiled and edited by
Clinton Detweiler - Director

Copyright 1974
Revised 1979
Second Revision 1991

by

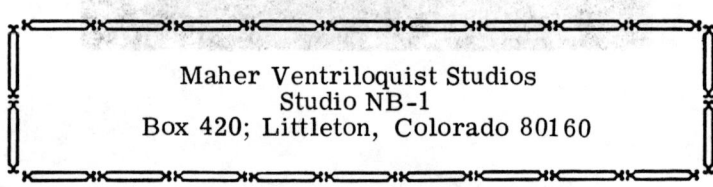

Maher Ventriloquist Studios
Studio NB-1
Box 420; Littleton, Colorado 80160

See the complete line of ventriloquist supplies, dialogue books, puppets, and professional ventriloquist figures. Ask your dealer or order a catalog ($2.00) from the above address.

Printed in the United States of America

ISBN 0-686-20905-2

"Hi! I'm 'Friendly Freddie', and I'll be your guide for the next 64 fun-filled pages. Follow me for an exciting venture into the fascinating subject of Ventriloquism... with ten easy-to-understand lessons.

"And it's ALL in this little book which I call, 'Ventriloquism in a Nutshell'. Are you ready? Okay, here we go!"

Illustrations and cartoons by Mr. David J. Miller, professional ventriloquist from Portland, Oregon. Mr. Miller was the 1974 recipient of the NAAV "Outstanding Ventriloquial Artist" Special Award for his outstanding contribution to the art of Ventriloquism through illustrative art.

## PREFACE

Ventriloquism - or the art of "throwing the voice". An ancient art which has increased in popularity through the ages. In today's modern world we find hundreds of persons from every walk of life using ventriloquism to entertain, instruct, and communicate.

The single most powerful factor the ventriloquist has working for him is this: The listener wants to hear EVERY WORD the vent figure (dummy) has to say! The percentage of dialogue retained in the mind of the listener is very high when compared with that retained from a lecture or speech given without any type of visual aid. And, among the list of visual aid tools, the ventriloquial figure stands alone - at the very top of the list.

For entertainment alone, ventriloquism is always certain success. This art combines the warmth and magnetism of puppetry; the mystery and wonder of magic; the fun and excitement of show business. Best of all, ventriloquism is a hobby or profession which requires a very small investment of time and dollars. Yet, this simple skill is potentially very profitable. High profits from a small investment; a combination that is hard to beat.

Contrary to what you may have been told, learning ventriloquism is well within the ability of any man, woman, or child who will devote a reasonable amount of time to the art. And, it can be learned easily and quickly at home in a reasonably short period of time. A normal speaking voice and the desire to learn; these two requirements are the only ones the future vent needs to provide.

Many vent books, records, and other instructional helps have been offered through the years. We feel this book, "Ventriloquism in a Nutshell", is one of the best concise introductory studies of the subject. The book is designed to introduce the reader to all the basics of the art of ventriloquism in a fun and orderly step-by-step program.

Mr. Clinton Detweiler, a professional ventriloquist and magician; also the Director of Maher Ventriloquial Studios and President of the North American Association of Ventriloquists, was the editor and compiler of this book. "Ventriloquism in a Nutshell" is a revised version of the Maher Introductory Course through which thousands have learned to "throw their voice".

And, what others have done, you too, can do!

- "Friendly Freddie"

* * * * * * * * * * * * * * * * * * * * * * * *

\* \* \* \* \* \* \* \* \* \* \* \* \* \* \* \* \* \* \* \* \* \* \* \* \*

### NEED HELP? ASSISTANCE IS AVAILABLE!

I suppose everyone has SOME question about ventriloquism. As a special personal service to ALL readers of this book, Maher Ventriloquist Studios and their professional staff will answer (or try to answer) any question you might have on the subject of ventriloquism.

Your question might concern some area of the following lessons; it might concern your need for routines or supplies; it may be a trivia question or just the opposite - a serious research question. Any and all questions are welcome and will be promptly answered. There is NO CHARGE for this service and you will be under absolutely no obligation to Maher Studios, but please do include a self-addressed stamped return envelope with your question.

## CONTENTS

Preface .................................... 5

Help and Assistance ......................... 6

How To Use This Book ....................... 9

LESSONS:

    One    - Our Voice Mechanism ............. 11

    Two    - Breath Streams and Voice Contrast. 15

    Three - Your Most Important Tool ......... 23

    Four  - Ventriloquial Mouth Position ....... 29

    Five  - Ventriloquial "Dummies" .......... 33

    Six    - Lifelike Animations ............... 43

    Seven - Sound Substitutions (Part 1) ........ 47

    Eight - Sound Substitutions (Part 2) ........ 53

    Nine  - Sound Substitutions (Part 3) ........ 57

    Ten    - What Now? ...................... 61

For Your Further Study ....................... 64

Maher Ventriloquist Studios
Studio NB-1
Box 420; Littleton, Colorado 80160

"Hey Roger, I think they got our suitcases mixed up."

## HOW TO USE THIS BOOK

CONGRATULATIONS to you on your decision to learn the wonderfully exciting art of Ventriloquism. It is a wonderful accomplishment and after you have learned ventriloquism it is something you will always have and no one can take it away from you. People will be amazed and entertained if you do it well. And this newly developed skill will hold tremendous possibilities for you. It can be used to entertain, teach, sell, illustrate, dramatize, and on and on. The ways in which ventriloquism can be used are limited only by our small imaginations!

"VENTRILOQUISM IN A NUTSHELL" is a short, simple home study plan. It is condensed from a portion of the Maher Master 30 Lesson Professional Course. "Nutshell" explains the basics of ventriloquism including Breath Control, Voice Placement, Lip Control, Sound Substitution, and Vent Figure Manipulation among other subjects. Each subject is explained in a systematic step-by-step manner.

Thousands of artistic and witty people (for I believe that it takes those qualities to be attracted to the art of ventriloquism) write Maher Studios saying that they have always been fascinated with ventriloquism and wanted to learn the art. For many, this book, "Ventriloquism in a Nutshell", meets their needs with no further training necessary. Others, wishing to develop their talent and skill even further, decide to enroll in the professional course which teaches in depth ALL areas of the art. Just as the title implies, this is a nutshell set of instructions; many in-depth subjects and explanations are omitted purposely to avoid any possible confusion or distraction.

Years ago it was my privilege to be among the many successful graduates of the Maher Professional Home Study Course. Since I personally learned the art of ventriloquism by the Maher method, I can assure you from my own experience that it is a practical, workable learning method. The following chapters will very clearly explain and illustrate the secrets of ventriloquism.

Ventriloquism, like any art, takes some effort to learn. It will be easy and fun if you will read these lessons thoughtfully, giving each lesson your full attention. Then, when you are certain that you understand the instructions, do the exercises as outlined. Repeat them often until you have mastered them. Yes, PRACTICE will be necessary for you to accomplish the art of ventriloquism. We suggest 10 - 30 minutes of daily study and practice. Many opportunities for practice may be incorporated into your daily work routine quite easily. All the effort and attention you give the lessons will be rewarding. Your time will prove to be well invested. You will find the lessons to be easy and FUN!

So, with the help of "Friendly Freddie", let's get started now.

Clinton Detweiler - Director<br>Maher Ventriloquist Studios

* * * * * * * * * * * * * * * * * * * * * * *

## LESSON ONE - OUR VOICE MECHANISM

Our voice mechanism is one of the most wonderful of all creations; the most marvelous of all INSTRUMENTS. How about the flute, piano, pipe organ, etc? Your voice surpasses any of them. In natural speech there are many things we do naturally and yet are not conscious of doing; in fact, we have always done it since we were a baby.

To be a ventriloquist we must KNOW WHAT WE ARE DOING. The reason is because we are going to have to change some of our methods of speaking. The tone of our voice will also be changed for ventriloquism. As you know, the ventriloquist, to be a good one, must have a different tone of voice for his ventriloquial voice than he has for his own natural speaking voice. Most important of all, he must SPEAK WITHOUT MOVING HIS LIPS.

Now, let us introduce you to the inside of your mouth. Get a small mirror and a flashlight. Now stick your tongue out of your mouth and look at the very back of your throat. Shine the flashlight toward the back of your throat so that you can see better. Got it? Okay. Now, with your mouth opened WIDE and looking inside, say Ah-Ah-Ah---. What happened? At the back of your mouth you see an ARCH. It is called the Palentine arch. Hanging in the middle is a little fleshy muscle. It is called your UVULA. Before you said "Ah" it was hanging down relaxed from the top of the arch. As soon as you said "Ah" it raised to the top of the roof of your mouth. Why? To allow your flow of breath and sound to flow out of your mouth in as wide a passage as possible.

Say "Oh-Oh" What is the reaction of your uvula? It's the same as before isn't it? Now put the mirror and light down and say the "a" sound that is in the word "shay". This time say the word "shay" a few tones higher than your natural speaking voice and say it more UP IN YOUR NOSE. Experiment with it until you can feel breath coming through your NOSE. In fact, your nose should feel a slight tingling or some vibration in it.

TRY IT AGAIN! First say "Ah" with your open throat and then say each of the vowels (a-e-i-o-u). As you say these sounds while using the flashlight and mirror again, look into your mouth and watch your uvula (like a little acrobat) raise up high to let each sound escape from your throat.

Try it again on each of these vowel sounds: "a e i o u".

To PROVE it to yourself, place your hand before your mouth when you say each of these sounds. You will feel the breath coming from your throat with each of these sounds.

RIGHT? Now say them again, placing your hand under your NOSE. Do you feel any breath coming through your nose? No. Only one stream can be felt and it is coming through your mouth only.

To speak ventriloquially we want you to get the sound well up into your NOSE. You will be able to check yourself to know if you have your voice PLACED CORRECTLY for ventriloquism, by the same method; by putting your hand under your nose. When you are speaking correctly for the ventriloquist voice you should feel most of your breath stream coming through your nose and a little coming through your mouth.

Now let us find the right place in your throat and head to speak VENTRILOQUIALLY. Go back to the "Ah" sound we first talked about in this lesson. Say it as follows:

Ex. 1
```
ah   ah   ah   ah   ah   ah
ha   ha   ha   ha   ha   ha
ah   ha   ah   ha   ah   ha
```

That's enough of that - let's try something different now. Say the sound "N" - and the word "None".

Repeat it:   None   none   none   none

What did your tongue do on the sound of "n"? You won't have to look inside your mouth to SEE. You can FEEL it. Your tongue touched the roof of your mouth. While repeating the word "none" several times, feel in front of your mouth. Where is the breath? There is indeed "none". Now feel under your nose while saying "none". That's correct, the breath is coming through your nose. Why? As your tongue touched the roof of your mouth it forced the breath AND sound up through the nose while it blocked any passage of breath and sound through your mouth.

Now say the sound "NG" -- as in the word "siNGiNG." Separate the sound of the word and say it alone. Start with the complete word - then sound the "NG" found in the word:

siNG-iNG    siNG-iNG    siNG-iNG

Now repeat it and while HOLDING the "NG" tone feel your nose. Do you feel it VIBRATE? Good. One additional point, on the "NG" tone what does your tongue do? Notice that it is the MIDDLE part of the tongue that presses against the roof of your mouth. This will be an important point in another lesson.

Go back to Exercise 1 with the "ah" sound. Repeat the exercise. Feel your throat with your hand. Do you feel it vibrate or tingle? Then you know that you are talking with an open throat, the way it was when you looked in your mouth while using the flashlight. Say the word shay-shay-shay- and feel the front of your throat. Can you feel the vibration in the throat? Now I want you to say that same word up in your nose where you have been saying the "N" sound and the "NG" sound. Raise it higher in tone until you can't feel it in your throat at all but NOW you can feel the vibration in your nose.

Keep doing this until you can FEEL it in your nose. Say it higher in TONE than you would say it in your natural speaking voice and "talk in your nose".

Ex. 2    shay    shay    shay    shay
         shay    shay    shay    shay

If you can feel breath coming from your nose and some vibration in the nose, then YOU'VE GOT IT! That is where, in your vocal mechanism, you must talk ventriloquially. It would be well to go back to this lesson often to check yourself.

You have now learned the SECRET of correct ventriloquial VOICE PLACEMENT, and you are acquainted with the "magical" word SHAY. Make this word a part of your daily practice FROM NOW ON. And you need not be actually sitting down with these lessons to do this exercise; you can incorporate it into almost any part of your daily routine!

## LESSON TWO - BREATH STREAMS and VOICE CONTRAST

Place your fingers gently on your "Adam's Apple" and make the sound "zzzzzzzzz". Can you feel the buzz? You FEEL that because there are VOCAL CORDS inside of the throat. The "Larynx" is the real name of the "house" within your throat where the wonderful little organ that produces your voice is located.

The vocal cords are like little lips that form and make the voice. Perhaps at some time or other you have slit a piece of reed or grass and then blown through it. As the air passed through the reed it caused the reed to vibrate and make a sound. Just so with the little voice cords.

Your lungs, when filled with air, are like bellows that send the air up through these cords (or voice box) and then the voice is made.

When the voice gets to the back of the throat it is like coming to a gate or "arch" as we saw it to be in the first lesson. Then the little uvula lifts up so that there is plenty of room for the voice to come out. There are some sounds that need to go up through the nose instead of through the mouth. These sounds are "m", "n", and "ng". To direct the breath through the nose your uvula drops down like a curtain and this (with the help of the tongue) forces your breath through your nose.

Try this: Hum while holding the sides of your nose gently.

You should feel the vibrations of sound through the nose and cheeks. Now hum in a higher tone. The higher in tone you hum, the higher you will feel the vibrations in your head; even as high as your forehead. Try it.

Hum:  mum  mum  mmmmmmmmm

Now hum in a higher tone. Higher and still higher. Test it. Feel your nose. You will be able to feel it higher in your nose as you sing higher in tone. In fact, you may even feel it in your forehead.

There are pockets in your face, nose, and head which are filled with air like bellows. The sound bounces off of the bony parts in our face and head. The pockets make the sound "resonant" or in other words, they give your voice CARRYING power.

Because you want your voice as a ventriloquist to have carrying power let us do some exercises. (You need not try to keep your lips from moving at this point.)

Ex. 3
```
hum  hum  hum  bumble bee
hum  hum  hum
hum  hum  hum  bumble bee
```

(hum)  mmmmmmmmmmmmm
(Feel your face. Is it vibrating? It should be.)

Ex. 4

```
nnnnn  NIN nnnnn   NIN nnnnn
mmm    MIM mmm     MIM mmm
nnnnn  NAN nnnnn   NAN nnnnn
mmm    MAM mmm     MAM mmm
```

Now let us come back to "Shay shay shay". Say it until you can touch your nose and feel it vibrating almost as much as when you were saying the exercises with the humming sounds in them.

Keeping your voice placed correctly, let us say a group of words ventriloquially and TRY to keep your lips very still on every sound except these:

        F    V    P    B    M    W

The above letters are the most difficult for the ventriloquist. Don't worry about them now because later on you will have special help on them.

Ex. 5

| C | D | E |
|---|---|---|
| candy | daring | elate |
| cash | diary | else |
| carry | destiny | entrance |
| cracker | dialing | elastic |
| cricket | doesn't | electric |
| crier | dolly | eject |
| crinkle | don't | eloquent |

Now repeat the entire exercise checking yourself to be sure that you are saying the words not only with well controlled lips but also check to be certain that you are placing your voice well up into your nose. To check yourself, place your hand under your nose. Remember, you should feel breath coming from both your NOSE and MOUTH.

Okay? Now go over the exercise once more and this time in FRONT OF A MIRROR to see that you DO NOT MOVE YOUR LIPS.

## DIAGRAM SHOWING THE DIRECTION OF BREATH STREAMS

In the formation of "N" the tip of the tongue touches the roof of the mouth (see chart on the left), thus blocking the air stream so that the sound MUST be thrown up into the nasal speech cavity to escape through the nose.

In the formation of "shay", the tongue is lowered and uvula raised allowing the breath to pass both through the nose AND the mouth. The VENTRILOQUIST VOICE will combine these two breath streams. To check it, hold your hand before your nose and mouth. You should feel a stream of breath coming from both. (See chart on the right.)

NOTE: Individuals vary greatly in the amount of tingling or vibrations felt within the nose, face, and head while speaking ventriloquially. To some, this sensation is quite dramatic; to others it may be ever so slight.

To check the flow of the breath streams, use both the palm of your hand AND the back side of your hand. Often one side of the hand is more sensitive than the other and only by checking will you know which side is best for your testing purposes.

## VOICE CONTRAST

When working for CONTRAST between your own natural speaking voice and the voice you use ventriloquially, it is well to remember that even ONE TONE HIGHER than your natural speaking voice is sufficient to produce an acceptable difference between THE TWO VOICES. Of course, if you can raise your ventriloquial voice even higher, comfortably, this is helpful. But it is unnecessary to strain your voice in any way when you speak ventriloquially. It should be free and easy.

NOTE: It is easy to obtain a wide contrast in the voices by producing the ventriloquial voice in falsetto. Falsetto is an artificially produced high voice that extends above the normal range of the full voice. Using a falsetto vent voice WILL STRAIN the vocal cords, and although some ventriloquists do use a falsetto ventriloquial voice, it certainly is NOT recommended.

Although everyone has a different voice range, the natural voice from an open throat is LOW as compared to the ventriloquial voice which you will "throw" more to the FRONT OF YOUR MOUTH AND UP THROUGH YOUR NOSE. The vent voice in most cases should be higher than your natural speaking voice. (The exceptions might be with the vent who has a very high pitched natural voice who would then use a ventriloquial voice in a lower range.) But - if you use a lower pitched ventriloquial voice you risk losing some or all of the unique tonal quality produced by the resonance chambers.

When speaking ventriloquially, you are throwing your voice up into the same place that you normally produce the sounds "m", "n", and "ng". These sounds are the resonant sounds. This placing of your voice up into the combination of your NOSE and FRONT OF MOUTH gives it a QUALITY that is different from your own speaking voice. For that reason, you not only have a voice in the higher register, but you will have a different QUALITY in your voice. Because of this, you will have a distinct CONTRAST between voices...you can also obtain contrast by varying your tone, pitch, tempo, and volume. In other words, if you speak in a low tone at a normal speed, your ventriloquial voice can be higher in tone and faster in tempo. This method will give you excellent CONTRAST. Anything that is different in the two methods of speaking will help obtain contrast.

TRY THIS: Take a simple sentence such as, "This is the voice very low." First, say this sentence in your natural speaking voice at your natural tone level. Second, say the sentence one tone higher, "This is the sentence one tone higher."

Repeat the above sentence again and again, each time LISTEN for the first word of the sentence and say it, with the entire sentence, one tone higher. Use the musical scale to set the tone just as you would in singing, "Do - Re - Mi - Fa - Sol - La - Ti - Do". Sing them first so that you HEAR them distinctly. Then SAY one word on one particular note. Next, TALK YOUR SENTENCE on each individual tone level. In other words, say a sentence on the tone level of the lower "Do". Then say the same sentence on the same tone level as "Re", etc. Continue up the scale one note higher each time, until you find it strains your voice. Stop on the tone BEFORE that happens. This then will be the maximum ventriloquial voice level you should try to achieve.

Each time you start your sentence, be certain that your first word is clearly on that particular tone before you continue the sentence. If you have a piano or musical instrument, you can PLAY that particular note first and then TALK (not sing) on that note of music. If you have a tape or cassette recorder, use it. In this way you will hear the VARIETY and will then be able to produce contrasts in your speech, the same as you do in singing.

In conclusion on the subject of voice contrast, listen carefully to speakers of every type. Notice in what ways they use their voices and what makes them effective. The popular (or irritating, depending upon your point of view) TV cartoons have a WIDE variety of voice types. Listen to some of them; try to mimic them. It is a good vocal exercise. And from these observations you will learn a great deal, especially in the light of what you are learning from this "nutshell" study of ventriloquism!

"Not, 'punch the line'! I said, 'read the punch line'!"

# Who can learn?

Right here we must take the time to explain that Ventriloquism does NOT take some "trick voice" or freak voice or split personality as is sometimes implied. Neither is there any special little "gimmick" that you slip into your mouth that enables you to throw your voice as is often implied in some cleverly worded advertisements.

**1.**      **2.**      **3.**

ANYONE can learn to be a ventriloquist IF they have:

## 1. A normal speaking voice
## 2. The desire to learn
## 3. Proper instruction

That's right, these are the only three requirements. Why, you ask, if ventriloquism is so simple, are there so few ventriloquists? Good question. And the answer is this - most people do not meet the second requirement named above. Most people would LIKE to learn ventriloquism, and even though they may have had a secret desire from their youth to learn, they are too busy, or lack the desire (or courage) to actually try.

We'll not pretend to fool you - ventriloquism DOES require practice...and more practice...and MORE practice. But, can you think of any true skill that can be mastered without practice? Of course not. Skill does not come in a package with a ribbon around it. Skill is that unique part of yourself that must be discovered, developed, and delivered - otherwise it is valueless. Take heart, for although learning ventriloquism takes practice, only a few minutes a day will bring almost spectacular results. And here's the big surprise: Ventriloquism practice is FUN, FUN, FUN!

## LESSON THREE - YOUR MOST IMPORTANT TOOL

You have learned something about what produces sound. Now the tongue (your most important tool) "gets into the act". The tongue is one of the most important members of your complete voice mechanism. The tongue is especially important to the ventriloquist because the ventriloquist cannot use his lips as we all do in natural speech. Therefore, his words must be made INSIDE his mouth rather than on his lips.

Our tongue is a wonderful member. It flattens on some sounds, points its tip up behind the teeth on other sounds, humps up in the middle for other sounds, etc. All of this usually without you even realizing it. The only trouble is that without some training our tongue (like ourselves) gets a little lazy or careless. This causes our speech to become thick and hard to understand. The ventriloquist cannot have a lazy tongue. He therefore has to insist that his tongue do a better job than for most people. It cannot be lazy if he wishes to be articulate and easily understood.

That is why our lessons include the use of the VENTRIL-O-AID for some of the exercises. The VENTRIL-O-AID makes you speak with your teeth parted so you cannot possibly use your lips while speaking. It also forces your jaw to remain stationary while speaking. This is important since both the LIPS and the JAW must remain still while speaking in the ventriloquial voice.

Just as lifting weights builds the muscles of the body, so the use of the VENTRIL-O-AID builds and develops the dexterity of the tongue. While using the VENTRIL-O-AID, your tongue has to stretch farther than usual on such sounds as the ones normally made with the tip of the tongue. Also on the sounds requiring the tongue to touch the roof of your mouth and the sounds that call for your tongue to touch behind your teeth.

When you have done some practicing with the VENTRIL-O-AID and then do the same ventriloquial exercises WITHOUT the VENTRIL-O-AID, you will find it easier to use your tongue efficiently. And you will depend less upon your lips for ventriloquial speech. So we cannot over-emphasize the importance of the use of the VENTRIL-O-AID.

VENTRIL-O-AID:

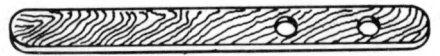

Let me remind you that the VENTRIL-O-AID is for PRACTICE ONLY; in fact, you won't be using it always but it will help exercise your tongue. With it you will be forced to speak without using your lips.

NOTE: If you do not own a VENTRIL-O-AID, you may substitute a pencil in it's place. However, the pencil is a bit awkward and the use of the VENTRIL-O-AID is recommended.

VENTRIL-O-AIDS ARE NOW AVAILABLE FREE from Maher Ventriloquist Studios (address on page 2). Simply send a stamped, self-addressed return envelope with your request for a "Free Ventril-o-aid".

This, as all other opportunities available from Maher Studios, will be valid indefinitely. Why wait? Send your letter now.

With the following exercise, place the VENTRIL-O-AID on edge between your teeth so that the two ends of it are OUTSIDE of your lips. Okay, let's go!

Ex. 6

| K | L | T | D |
|---|---|---|---|
| kissing | letter | tea | dearly |
| keel | lettuce | tease | door |
| knolling | licking | tearing | dish |
| kicking | lottery | taxi | detail |
| kidding | lolling | tasting | dunce |
| kidney | locking | tattling | decently |
| khaki | lining | tattoo | dethrone |

Now take the VENTRIL-O-AID out of your mouth and say those same words ventriloquially. Now repeat the complete exercise again, with the VENTRIL-O-AID and without.

Check yourself:
(1) Are you placing your voice correctly?
(2) Can you feel more breath coming from your nose than from your mouth?
(3) Look into the mirror.
(4) Are you keeping your lips still?

On the next exercise pay special attention to having your ventriloquial voice sound different from your own natural speaking voice. Have it at least two or three tones HIGHER. (You might want to experiment with a LOWER voice if your natural voice is high.) Don't strain. Speak as much higher in tone as possible and still have it feel comfortable. Remember, now you are working to make the two voices SOUND DIFFERENT. Try to keep the lips as still as possible except for the "m" and the "p".

Ex. 7

| NATURAL VOICE: | VENTRILOQUIAL VOICE: |
| --- | --- |
| You. | You. |
| Yes. | No. |
| Who? | You. |
| Is it you? | Yes. |
| Are you certain? | Yes, you heard what I said. |
| Talk a little higher. | Shall I talk like this? |
| Don't strain. | I'm not. |

| | |
|---|---|
| You moved your lips on "m". | I know, I can't help it. |
| You moved your mouth on "p". | You think so? |
| Yes, but keep practicing. | I know. I know. |
| Let's rest. | Okay. Good idea! |

Continual practice and review is important and necessary if your learning is to be successful. So even though you are now ready to proceed to lesson four, be certain to repeat the exercises from previous lessons on a regular basis. Especially important are the exercises on voice placement and the exercises with the VENTRIL-O-AID.

Ventriloquism is a SKILL that is developed through practice as well as study. Students who try to get by with as little practice as possible are only cheating themselves!

"That's the last time you're gonna put words in my mouth!"

## LESSON FOUR - VENTRILOQUIAL MOUTH POSITION

Now we're moving right ahead but I want to talk to you about your correct ventriloquial mouth position. Put your teeth together as though you were going to BITE into a piece of meat. Now feel between your teeth with your fingers. Your upper teeth are down against - possibly over the lower ones. Isn't that right? Okay. Now, open your mouth just enough to part your teeth ever so slightly. There should be just enough room between your teeth to allow the sounds and words to pass through freely. (No more than 1/4 inch opening between upper and lower teeth.)

Let your jaw be RELAXED. In this way you can change the expression of your face; smile or look any way you wish (preferably as natural as possible), but the relaxed POSITION of your jaw remains the same for your CORRECT VENTRILOQUIAL MOUTH POSITION.

To start, I want you to review the humming exercises in lesson two. Next say the word "shay, shay, shay" and check yourself.

1. Can you feel most of the breath coming from your nose?
2. Is your mouth position correct?
3. Is your ventriloquial voice higher in tone than your own natural voice?

Okay. We are ready for more exercises and remember to check yourself on them every once in a while. Of course, when you are using the VENTRIL-O-AID this does not apply.

Ex. 8

1. Do this exercise WITH the VENTRIL-O-AID.
2. Do it ventriloquially WITHOUT the VENTRIL-O-AID.

| A | G | H | R |
|---|---|---|---|
| acknowledge | gold | hall | risen |
| action | golden | hat | rising |
| actual | goal | hull | riding |
| active | gilding | hasten | racial |
| alligator | giant | hostile | rhino |
| all clear | gladly | halter | reading |
| alike | gladden | halting | readily |
| altogether | gland | heating | receipt |
| around | glance | hand | recast |
| alliance | glassy | hither | reduce |

Now get your MIRROR out - or stand before a mirror and repeat the above exercise, watching your lips very carefully so that you don't move them. Count each time you DO move your lips and then try the exercise again seeing if you can reduce the count. Make a game of it!

Ex. 9   Using the same words, let's say one word in your natural speaking voice and then say the same word ventriloquially. LISTEN very carefully and try to have a real difference between the two voices.

Ex. 10

Here is a dialogue to practice a change of voice. "V" means ventriloquist and "F" means figure (ventriloquial figure). If you have a vent partner (dummy) it's time he came out of the suitcase. Set him on your knee and let him help you. Make him just as REAL and ALIVE as possible. Don't worry if you have to move your lips on the more difficult sounds. We'll master them later in the lessons.

V. What happened to the girl I saw you with in the hammock last summer?

F. Oh....we had a falling out!

V. I hear you are going to a new school now.

F. That's right.

V. How do you like school?

F. I like it CLOSED!

V. What are you taking up in school?

F. SPACE.

V. No, seriously, what are you TAKING?

F. Anything I can get my hands on!

V. Shame on you.

F. I was just kidding.

V. I'm glad. But tell me, what DO you like best?

F. RECESS!

V. Well, you like FOOTBALL don't you?

F. Yeah...but I had an accident at FOOTBALL PRACTICE.

V. Oh, that's too bad. What happened?

F. Well, at practice the coach yelled, "TACKLE THE DUMMY"

V. Yes......

F. Wow! They almost KILLED ME!

## LESSON FIVE - VENTRILOQUIAL "DUMMIES"

Ventriloquial figures (dummies) have a background almost as rich in tradition as human beings. History records that they were present in ancient Greece. For centuries they have been used in China and in many other countries as well. Of old they were found in the temples and took an active part in the religious ceremonies of many peoples. Down through the misty ages they have come, influencing the moods of men and stirring the emotions of those who stopped to look and listen. In our day a whole nation stops to listen and laugh at a ventriloquial figure.

The term "dummy" holds no sense of empty wooden-headedness whatsoever. It seems almost like their nationality to me. Perhaps their native country is in the whimsey of men's and women's hearts. The dummy is usually precocious and not impressed with anyone. He is like all children, not at all self-conscious. He owes no one anything, patronizes no one, holds no ill will toward anyone. Ventriloquial figures always seem to be a cross between fairy children and dwarfs with a little masculine or feminine sophistication thrown in. They have a "Puckish" quality, half grown up, half child; now naive, now worldly, at all times provocative. They are perpetually unpredictable - hence their charm. The audience is always their friend. The audience is always on their side.

A prominent writer on stage technique writes: "a deep, warm imagination is a necessary requisite for an actor." Pretending that there are two people before an audience, one the ventriloquist, and the other the "dummy", exchanging clever witticisms will only seem real when both parts are properly acted. The ventriloquist has his part to act and likewise the figure has his part.

True, part of the ventriloquist's acting ability and artistry is to bring the ventriloquial figure to life, but to make this possible the figure must have some fundamental qualities for the ventriloquist to get the most out of him. To properly carry out his share of the illusion, the ventriloquial figure must have winsomeness, individuality, expression, and a lifelike appearance.

The ventriloquist's "dummy" is to the ventriloquist what a musical instrument is to the musician. The musician plays his music through his instrument. The instrument through which the ventriloquist plays his wit and humor is his ventriloquial figure. The best musician cannot bring forth fine music through a poor instrument, likewise the ventriloquist cannot bring forth hearty laughter nor properly display his technique through an inadequate ventriloquial figure. For this reason, your choice of a figure will be an IMPORTANT one to you.

Puppets, marionettes, and ventriloquial figures are all of the same family. Their craft is purely of the stage and theater. When the ventriloquist attempts to project the illusion of another living personality, through his manipulation of a wooden figure (lending it his wit, action, and voice); whether he is in an auditorium, appearing before several hundred people; or perhaps before the TV camera performing to an audience of millions; or just amusing a few friends in someone's humble home, he is engaging in the art of the theater. To do this successfully he must have a ventriloquial figure that has that essential theatrical quality.

If you are a ventriloquist, or when you become one, you will be working in the field of the arts and crafts. To be a good craftsman, you need the very BEST equipment available for your work. Preferably, you should purchase your equipment from persons or firms whose primary business is ventriloquism.

The success of such a supplier depends entirely upon YOUR success as a ventriloquist, and they will take a personal interest in your effort to select the proper equipment for your use. Quite likely you will be doing business by mail. Be certain your supplier guarantees customer satisfaction on all items sold.

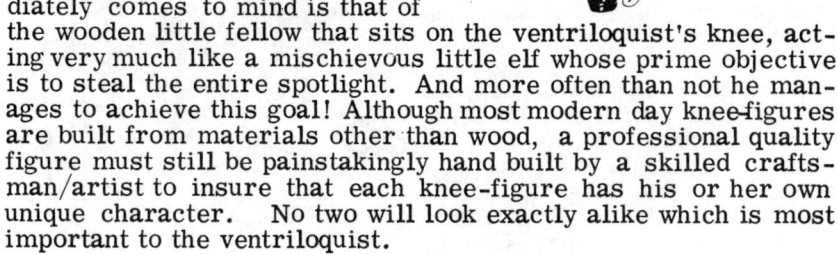

Mention a "ventriloquist dummy" and the character that immediately comes to mind is that of the wooden little fellow that sits on the ventriloquist's knee, acting very much like a mischievous little elf whose prime objective is to steal the entire spotlight. And more often than not he manages to achieve this goal! Although most modern day knee-figures are built from materials other than wood, a professional quality figure must still be painstakingly hand built by a skilled craftsman/artist to insure that each knee-figure has his or her own unique character. No two will look exactly alike which is most important to the ventriloquist.

Animal or bird characters are favorites of all audiences, especially children. It's almost as if the puppet radiates some mystical magnetism that reaches out and draws the attention and hearts of the children. Psychologists and other therapists sometimes use animal characters in therapy sessions with children. The inhibited child will often open up and talk to the animal (or bird) puppet after all other methods of communication have failed. The ventriloquist puppet is capable of return communication which is a great advantage to the therapist.

Animal characters also lend themselves to a great amount of ACTION and comical contortions. Children love the many zany stunts provided by a character such as the mischievous crow pictured above. But I'll let you in on a secret, adults enjoy the performance just as much (or more) than the children!

The types of ventriloquial figures are endless; limited only by the imagination of their creators. The Grumpett pictured below is a ventriloquial variation of a full body hand puppet. The Grumpett is wonderfully effective with many head and body movements. ACTION plus WORDS - a fantastic combination!

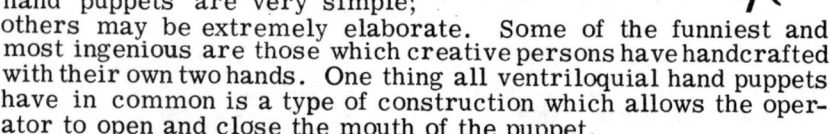

Creativety is the key to every successful ventriloquist act. Some of the most successful professional vents use a partner which they created themselves. The majority, however, prefer to enlist the services of an experienced craftsman whose work is of proven quality and audience appeal.

The simplest of all puppets is the hand puppet which slips over the hand. These may be made from an old sock or purchased from the large selection available commercially. Some hand puppets are very simple; others may be extremely elaborate. Some of the funniest and most ingenious are those which creative persons have handcrafted with their own two hands. One thing all ventriloquial hand puppets have in common is a type of construction which allows the operator to open and close the mouth of the puppet.

Sometimes the very best characters are those that just "happened". The builder starts with a variety of odds and ends plus the willingness to experiment and create. The end result may be as much a surprise to the builder as to the observer! Several of the ventriloquial characters on these pages were "born" in this very manner.

Hopefully this chapter will broaden your concept of ventriloquist "dummies". Although the knee-figure remains the most popular of the ventriloquist side-kicks, the variety of characters certainly is not limited to that one type. The active ventriloquist will own several vent figures of various types. This variety of characters adds color and versatility to his performing capabilities. Two or more figures may possibly be used simultaneously.

In choosing a ventriloquial figure there are several important points to remember. Select a character type which appeals to you - you cannot perform successfully with a character you do not ENJOY being with; it just will not work. Also try to choose the TYPE of figure which is suitable for the VOICE and PERSONALITY you have developed for it. As we have noted, many types of ventriloquial figures are available to you; however, your repertoire of voices probably will determine the number of different characters you will own and use.

(All of the ventriloquial characters pictured in this book were selected from the many pictured in the Maher Catalog.)

Your hand within the ventriloquial hand puppet provides form for the puppet as well as the important mouth operation. Not only does the mouth open and close, but the flexibility of the head allows a variety of facial expressions to be formed quite effectively, simply by twisting or stretching the head from within.

And now for some additional exercise which will enable you to proceed with YOUR ventriloquial study!

Ex. 11  STRETCH YOUR TONGUE out of your mouth. Make it long and pointed; the end should be as small as a thick lead pencil. Now repeat this exercise ten times. That's an excellent exercise for you. Get your mirror out and watch yourself. Be sure to make the tip of your tongue tiny. This will help make your tongue more obedient to you. It will always have a little more work than usual to do for you as a ventriloquist because of the work your lips do NOT do. Now let's use the VENTRIL-O-AID to follow up that exercise. With the VENTRIL-O-AID in place, say the following set of words.

Ex. 12

| I | L | T | O |
|---|---|---|---|
| inkling | lines | taking | older |
| indeed | listing | talking | oleo |
| incur | light | tangle | orange |
| into | lighter | tangerine | oddity |
| illustrate | likely | tall | octave |
| in-and-in | lilting | tail | oily |
| increase | lily | toil | okay |
| indecisive | linkage | talon | one |
| include | lining | tank | onion |
| individual | linen | toot | oozing |

Now let us do some practice the fun way. DO NOT use the VENTRIL-O-AID. Take your "pal" on your knee and talk to him.

Try for: Good contrast between the two voices.
  Act as though two people are talking together,
    reacting toward one another.
  Control your lips as much as possible.
  Is your mouth position correct for ventriloquism?
  If not, review its explanation in lesson four.

Ex. 13

F. Say, it's good to get out of that suitcase.

V. Well, you're not afraid of the dark, are you?

F. No - but it's nicer out.

V. Why do you feel that way?

F. Oh - I can see what's going on.

V. I suppose so.

F. If I stay in there, I'll be talking to myself, and people will think I'm CRAZY.

V. Oh, I don't think so. You don't have to be crazy to talk to yourself.

F. No - but it HELPS!

V. A ventriloquist talks to himself.

F. See what I mean!

V. How is school coming?

F. It's coming but I'm GOING.

V. You must learn to enjoy school.

F. The trouble is, I have a DUMB teacher. She sure can't know much!

V. What makes you think "she can't know much"?

F. She's always ASKING QUESTIONS.

V. I think you should do more home work. Would you like me to help you?

F. Sure.

V. Okay. Can you give me an example of the THREE VERB FORMS - indicative, interrogative, and imperative?

F. Well?

V. Come on. Quit stalling...try it: INDICATIVE

F. Jack is sick.

V. Yes, that's correct. Now: INTERROGATIVE.

F. Is Jack sick?

V. Right!.....IMPERATIVE.

F. Sick 'em Jack!!

V. Here's a problem for you. Name the Presidents of the United States.

F. You're kidding!

V. No, I'm serious.

F. That is IMPOSSIBLE; there are too many.

V. When I was your age, I could name ALL the Presidents.

F. Yeah? When you were MY age there was only WASHINGTON!

    Practice becomes a great deal of fun when you, with your ventriloquial pal, go through a humorous dialogue together. At some future date you may perform this same, now familiar dialogue before your family and friends. Their laughter and applause will inspire you to even greater achievement.

    When you, as a successful ventriloquist have finished a performance, and bow off the stage in the white spotlight, to the surge of tremendous applause coming up to you from a large, excited, and admiring audience - you have won a THRILL that cannot be known until you have experienced it.

## RULES FOR SUCCESSFUL ROUTINES

1) Second best laugh gag at the beginning of routine.

2) Best laugh at finish.

3) Act should always be built to a climax at the finish.

4) Always leave on a BIG laugh.

5) Routine should maintain a fast pace. The more brisk and sparkling the better. (However, you should always wait sufficiently for the laughs.)

6) Encore should top the routine with quick gags and good laughs.

7) Short, concise, and WITTY answers by the vent figure set a fast pace to your act.

8) Figure's remarks should always get laughs as much as possible.

9) The dialogue should have reasonable continuity.

10) The goal should always be to attain the greatest number of laughs with the fewest number of words.

# Distant Ventriloquism

The sound of a voice coming from a far distant point is where the idea of "throwing the voice" originated. This type of SOUND ILLUSION is more difficult to create than the Near Ventriloquism illusion and is less commonly used by performers.

Amazing effects may be achieved through the skillful use of Distant Ventriloquism. Voices from closets, another room, the attic, the basement - these are all forms of Distant Ventriloquism.

## Combining the two. . . .

Some form of Distant Ventriloquism is often used in combination with Near Ventriloquism, however. For example: a voice on the telephone or a muffled voice from within the suitcase; these are common popular adaptations of the Distant Voice.

While all forms of Ventriloquism require a degree of acting on the part of the performer, Distant Ventriloquism requires a great deal of acting. This booklet will deal primarily with the first and easiest form of ventriloquism...also one of the most practical and effective.

By following the simple instructions in this booklet, you too, will soon be able to surprise your friends with your ability to make a puppet "talk".

## LESSON SIX - LIFELIKE ANIMATIONS

Lifelike movements of the ventriloquial figure are VERY important. The little fellow sitting upon your knee must appear ALIVE. Work hard to keep him animated; avoid any "woodenlike' stare. He can say something that he "thinks" is pretty clever and look at the audience after he says it to give the effect of "I really told him that time, didn't I?"

When we are excited, our movements are quick and animated. Let his be also. Keep him moving a little. As you set him upon your knee, grasp the headstick and turn his head towards you. He should look at you while he is talking to you but do not turn his head so far that only the back of his head is visible to the audience. Always operate him as though he is not only conscious of you but the audience also. You, the ventriloquist, must keep these same points in mind for yourself as well.

Suppose someone says to you (even in your own living room), "I didn't know that you were a ventriloquist." Let your little pal answer them. He can say, "I didn't either - I see him moving his lips every time I speak." And you could scold him and tell him to "be polite". You must insist on some "respect from him". He can mock you and say in a kidding way, "Yes SIR"; "No SIR"; "I'll watch it SIR!" Then let him turn to the one who started the conversation and say to him (aside), "See how I have to humor him!" You can then say "What?" to which he replies, "Yes sir!"

When he talks he can move his head around. He can also move it up and down a little, especially if he is surprised; let him lift it up just high enough so that it does not show the separation between the body and head.

If you sing a duet, when you are singing your part and hit a high note, let him lift his head high, seeming to stretch his neck while looking at you. This will get a laugh from your audience every time.

If you have him sit on the edge of your knee, not too far back, you will find that you can make his body move slightly every time you move the headstick which will make him more lifelike. Also, the arms and legs will then take on a slight movement of their own. This again, is more lifelike.

There are several positions which the ventriloquist may assume while operating the vent figure. The one most often pictured is a standing ventriloquist, one foot upon a chair and the "dummy" upon his knee. If the ventriloquist is performing from a stage or raised platform, he or she might work from a sitting position, again with the vent figure sitting upon the knee.

Most vents prefer to work from the standing position although many do not feel that it is in good taste to prop one foot upon a chair while performing. This leaves two alternatives. 1) The figure can be held during the entire performance. This allows excellent movability; the vent can even walk to and fro if desired. But holding the figure while standing does require the use of both hands at all times which limits the ventriloquist's ability to gesture, etc. It can also be tiring. Perhaps a better method would be to, 2) Set the figure upon a stand (see sketch) which allows the ventriloquist to freely stand before the audience and operate the figure with ease in a professional style.

A little practice and experimentation will determine the manner in which you hold your partner while performing. Choose the position that allows you to be the most comfortable and relaxed...and effective.

When "speaking" the mouth of the ventriloquial figure should move with almost every syllable of every word you "put into his mouth". So, now is a good time to do some exercises that will help you master syncronization. His mouth must be syncronized with the words you speak for him; one of the very IMPORTANT things you do to build the illustration that he is REAL and ALIVE. This illustration (or illusion) must be believable. (You've watched a movie or TV show where the words were out of syncronization with the pictures - how disgusting; almost fake! NEVER allow this to happen to your performance.)

Remember: if he ACTS real and you have a reasonable difference between the voice you use for him and your own natural speaking voice, the audience will become so interested in watching your pal that they will forget to watch YOUR mouth.

In the following exercise you are going to learn the number of times you need to move his mouth on each syllable. The numbers are indicated below each word.

Ex. 14

V. Is school becoming any more enjoyable?

F. No, the tea/cher is still pick/ing on me.
   1    1    2    1  1    2    1  1

V. What's the trouble now?

F. Well, the oth/er day she ac/cused me of cheat/ing.
   1   1    2   1   1    2     1  1    2

V. CHEATING? That's a very serious thing to accuse you of.

F. Yeah, isn't it?
   1     2  1

V. Why yes! I'd make her PROVE it.

F. Well, yes...that's the trouble.
   1    1      1    1    2

V. What do you mean?

F. SHE DID!
   1    1

Now, go back and review your lessons from the very beginning. In fact, I wish you would review often. If you do, you will find it to be very rewarding. It will help you accomplish the art of ventriloquism that much FASTER.

To be a good pianist, one must practice. To be a good singer, dancer, or actor, one must practice. There is no accomplishment without effort, a willingness to devote ourselves to it, and to discipline ourselves.

VENTRILOQUISM is a FUN art. Determine to be the BEST!! Make your family and friends proud of you and you will find it so very worth while. You will be sharing fun and having it too.

## LESSON SEVEN - SUBSTITUTION SOUNDS (Part 1)

"TH" is a breath sound. It requires no lip movement whatsoever. Try it. Say: "Throw, throw, throw." NO LIP MOVEMENT is necessary, correct? So we are going to substitute the speech sound of the "TH" for the speech sound of the "F" every time we have to use "F" in ventriloquist speech. At first it may not be exactly the same, but when you slip it into a sentence it will never be noticed. Many of us slur some of our speech. We shouldn't, but we do and people are accustomed to it. So if a little guy or gal sitting on your knee does it, no one will mind.

Perhaps this is the proper time for a further comment concerning the substitution sounds you will be learning in this and the following two lessons. Although we will be teaching you substitution letters and sounds, you should (as quickly as possible) learn to "think" the letter being substituted FOR and not the letter or sound you are using as the substitute. LISTEN CAREFULLY as you pronounce the substitution. Try, over and over and over...and over, to make the substitution sound exactly the same as the original sound. And with practice, you'll be surprised to find that IT CAN BE DONE! Obviously, it is possible to learn to form all the difficult letters with your tongue rather than your lips; you've watched other ventriloquists speak without moving their lips, and if they can do it, so can YOU.

A tape or cassette recorder will prove a valuable help as you practice your substitution sounds. Listen carefully to your speech. Is it distinct? Is it clear? Ask a family member or friend to listen to the recording WITHOUT hearing you first. Can they understand what was being said? Yes - great! No - why not?

Okay, back to the substitution sound for "f". Do you remember what it was? That's right, "th", so let's practice.

SUBSTITUTION SOUND FOR "F"

| fish | becomes | THish |
| fair | " | THar |
| fine | " | THine |

LET'S TAKE SOME SENTENCES

Ex. 15

V. Did you go <u>fishing</u> today?

F. Yes, you should see the big <u>TH</u>ish I caught.

V. Did you go <u>far</u> to catch them?

F. No, it wasn't <u>TH</u>ar at all.

V. Was it a <u>fine</u> specimen?

F. Was it <u>TH</u>ine? It was terri<u>TH</u>ic!

Do you see how these sounds slip easily into speech and the substitution is hardly noticable at all?

We will now use almost the same substitution sound for "V" but there should be LESS force to the "th." We'll use the softer "th" sound found in the word "there." Try it: "there, there, there." Notice the difference between the softer "th" in "there" and the more forceful "TH" in "THrow?" Try it again. Be certain to form the sound of the "TH" and "th" with your tongue behind your upper teeth and do NOT form these sounds by placing your tongue between your upper and lower teeth as some people do for normal speech. Remember the difference between the soft "th" from the word "there" (used in place of the "V") and the more forceful "TH" from the word "THrow" (used in place of the "f"). It is very important that you use the correct substitute in the proper place if you expect your ventriloquial speech to sound clear and distinct to your listeners.

So, the substitution sound for "v" becomes a soft "th" spoken in place of the "v." You can easily make this sound without the use of your lips.

LET'S TRY IT!

Ex. 16

| vacant | becomes | thacant |
| very | " | thery |
| vastly | " | thastly |
| victory | " | thictory |
| village | " | thillage |

Now let's take some sentences with that same sound.

Ex. 17

Have you a vacant house next door?
Have you a thacant house next door?

I like her very much.
I like her thery much.

The soldiers won a victory yesterday.
The soldiers won a thictory yesterday.

Here's a tongue twister for you. Say it ventriloquially.

"Hey Friendly Freddie! Fancy finding this fragile gift from friend Vivian!"

Note: Some vents find that it is easier to make the usual "f" sound but to practice until they can make it with a still lip. In this manner the "f" requires no substitution. But I have found that it is easier to master the substitution than it is to master a still lip. Same is true of the "v" sound. Do whichever is easiest for you.

The "W" may be handled easily by using your lungs to place a short, breathy "huh" before the "w" in ventriloquist speech:

| walk | becomes | huhwalk |
| win  | "       | huhwin  |
| well | "       | huhwell |

Your lips will want to move to help form the "w". You must not let them! The "huh" sound provides the force lost without the help of your lips.

Here is an alternate method of making the "w" sound which you might find easier. It uses the "oo" sound (as in "boo") in place of the "w". Try it:

| walk | becomes | oo-alk |
| well | "       | oo-ell |
| wink | "       | oo-ink |

Did you find this substitution more to your liking? The important thing to remember is this: Use the substitution sounds which provide the most distinct true sound with the least lip movement. And once you decide which substitution you are going to use, STICK WITH IT. Trying first one and then another will only confuse you and you'll produce neither one with your best possible effort.

OKAY, LET'S PRACTICE WITH SOME SENTENCES

Was Willie climbing the wall?
Huhwas Huhwillie climbing the huhwall?
or
Oo-as Oo-illie climbing the oo-all?

Now try these:

Walking in the wilderness is wild.
Was my washing done well?
Words with "W" are not so wicked!

I tossed that last sentence at you to surprise you a bit! Notice that the letter "W" said alone presents another situation entirely. Actually, you are saying something to the effect of "double-you" which requires a "B" substitution. This is going to be explained in another chapter.

We are used to using our lips when saying the words with "w" but it really is not necessary. Again, practice before a mirror until your lips show no movement at all!

Using your sound substitutions as you have learned them, say the following words ventriloquially. It will take plenty of PRACTICE to REMEMBER to do it, so let's get busy. Get your pal out and let him sit upon your knee. He can help you and you know how he hates that suitcase. Besides, he may be lonesome!

HERE WE GO!

Ex. 19 ("WH" sound)

| where | what | when |
| wheel | wheat | wheeze |
| whelp | whip | white |

Now let's take some sentences with the "wh" sound in some of the words and be sure to say them the correct way for ventriloquism. Ready? Let's go!

Ex. 20

While waiting for the white ship I asked, why?
Have you heard a dog whine or a horse whinny?
Willie Whipple is in a wild whirl over Wilma.

Ex. 20 (continued)

> The whole white wholesome group.
> Bring your wicker basket to the wiener roast.
> Can you whittle while you whistle?

Now let's try another exercise to be certain we master this sound.

Ex. 21

| huhwa | watch | oo-a | watch |
|-------|-------|------|-------|
| huhwe | when  | oo-e | when  |
| huhwi | will  | oo-i | will  |
| huhwy | while | oo-y | while |
| huhwo | woke  | oo-o | woke  |
| huhwa | wait  | oo-a | wait  |
| huhwi | which | oo-i | which |
| huhwee | wheel | oo-ee | wheel |

Maybe that's not too easy at first. Give it plenty of practice. Did you do the entire exercise with the breathy "huh" sound before each "w" sound? Or were you using the "oo" substitution? In either case, how about trying it once more for good measure?

Let me take time out here to tell you the SECRET OF DISTINCT SOUND SUBSTITUTION. You must practice making all labial substitutions over and over and over until you are able to make them mechanically...without even thinking about what you are doing! This takes practice, practice, and MORE practice. When you are finally able to make all substitutions as a matter of habit, without thinking about what you're doing, an amazing thing happens. You'll stop thinking about what you're doing and you'll start LISTENING to the sound of what you're saying, and at that point YOUR WORDS WILL BECOME MORE CLEAR AND DISTINCT.

Amazing? Yes, indeed. Unfortunately, most people who have tried without success to become ventriloquists simply gave up before they had reached the point of mechanical sound substitution described above. So even though the substitute letters and sounds may sound awkward at first, don't become discouraged. They WILL work if only you give them (and yourself) a chance!

## LESSON EIGHT - SOUND SUBSTITUTION (Part 2)

Let's begin this lesson with some of the easier ventriloquist speech sounds and then we will finish up with some new sounds which need sound substitution for good ventriloquial speech.

Ex. 22

| S | SH | Y | Z |
|---|---|---|---|
| stare | shush | your | zander |
| staring | sheik | yet | zest |
| store | sheet | yeast | zestful |
| storing | sheer | yokel | zany |
| style | shawl | yard | zero |
| stylish | shear | yell | zebra |
| send | shekel | you | zink |
| sending | shiver | yawn | zone |
| scene | shilling | youth | zoo |
| secure | shirt | yippie! | zigzag |

How is the difference between your two voices? Be sure to work for a distinct difference. Remember our explanation in lesson 2; normally the ventriloquial voice should be higher in tone than yours and more nasal. Now run through exercise 22 saying each word first in your own natural speaking voice and then say the word ventriloquially. When you say the word in your natural voice, feel your throat. You should feel vibration in it. Now put your hand in front of your mouth. You should feel breath coming from your mouth.

Next, when you say the word ventriloquially, feel the bridge of your nose. Does it have some vibration in it? It should. Now put your hand under your nose. Do you feel breath coming from it as you speak? Also check your mouth while you speak ventriloquially. There should be only a small amount of breath coming from it and very little vibration in the throat.

Now, let's again get your pal out of the suitcase and let him help you with the exercises. Then, when you have finished, have another "talk" with him with the help of exercise 23.

"Why don't YOU read the parts marked 'Dummy'?"

Ex. 23

V. I've been reading a great deal about space ships and there have been several reports on TV.

F. Yeah...I notice it too.

V. I certainly hope all of this doesn't lead to war.

F. Me too!

V. Do you object to WAR?

F. Oh, I sure do.

V. Good, I'm glad to hear it.

F. Yeah - I HATE war.

V. Why do you hate war so much?

F. Well, war makes HISTORY doesn't it?

V. Indeed it does.

F. Well, I HATE HISTORY!!

Now let's learn the ventriloquial speech sound for the letter "M". Many ventriloquists use the letter "N" as a substitute for the letter "M". In other words, "million" becomes "nillion". You can use this if you wish but the "ng" sound is really better and far more realistic.

What do we mean by the "ng" sound? Say the word "song" and hold the tone at the end of the word. "Songggggggggg" Feel the position of your tongue against the roof of your mouth? Good - this is the way you produce the "ng" sound which we will substitute for the letter "m" in all words we say ventriloquially.

| Example: | Mary | becomes | Ngary |
|---|---|---|---|
| | more | " | ngore |
| | must | " | ngust |

In natural speech the "m" sound is made with the lips closing tightly, forcing the breath and sound through the nose. Often there will be some vibration felt on the closed lips as the "m" is said.

Try it. Say:  mmmmmm   mmmmmm   mmmmmm
                     mum         mum         mum

Ventriloquially, the tongue has to do the work for this sound and the lips do no work at all. Because some students ask what the "ng" sound is, let us analyze it. You probably make this sound hundreds of times a day in your normal speech. Here are some familiar words containing the "ng" sound. I want you to read them aloud - SLOWLY. Separate the "ng" sound in these words as you say them. LISTEN to the words and ask yourself, "What am I doing to make this "ng" sound?"

Here are the words:

        singing   -   siNGiNG
        swimming   -   swimmiNG
        yawning   -   yawniNG
        ding dong   -   diNG doNG
        king   -   kiNG

Okay. WHERE did you make the "ng" sound in your mouth? You pressed the middle/back portion of your tongue against the roof of your mouth, didn't you? Try it again. Notice that the sound could not come out through your mouth so it vibrated and carried up through your nose instead. So you now have discovered that you can indeed produce the sound of the letter "m" without using your lips at all. For that reason we will from this point on substitute the "ng" sound for the "m" in our ventriloquial speech. Since it is IMPOSSIBLE for the average person to make the sound of "M" WITHOUT the use of their lips, you will appear to be doing the impossible. One more SECRET of ventriloquism has now been revealed to you.

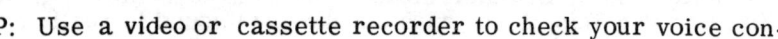

TIP: Use a video or cassette recorder to check your voice contrast and diction.

"Hey - that's ME!"

## LESSON NINE - SUBSTITUTION SOUNDS (part 3)

Let's take a quick review of the sounds "f", "v", and "w". Read lesson seven again to be certain that you are doing them correctly.

Ex. 24

| F | V | W |
|---|---|---|
| follow | velocity | water |
| fondness | vocal | wishful |
| footage | vocalize | wasteful |
| fountain | vocalizing | weight |
| food | vision | way |
| flying | visionary | western |
| flux | visualize | winning |
| flush | visualizing | won't |
| folded | vivid | wall |
| fishing | vividly | whoopee! |

Get the VENTRIL-O-AID out. You haven't used it for a long time but it will be a good exercise so that your tongue does not get lazy. Do ALL of exercise 24 with it.

Now place your pal on your knee. DON'T use the VENTRIL-O-AID this time. You say one word and have your pal repeat it after you. Sit in front of a mirror so that you are not only the performer but your own audience as well. Be a critical critic this time and if you are not satisfied with the ACT - demand an encore for improvement.

Now to overcome the troublesome "B". Our substitute sound for "b" will be "g".

| bats | becomes | gats |
| be | " | ge |
| ball | " | gall |
| best | " | gest |
| barn | " | garn |

IMPORTANT: BEFORE PROCEEDING ANY FURTHER, TURN BACK TO LESSON 7, page 47 AND REVIEW THE USE OF THE SUBSTITUTION LETTERS.

I sometimes hear students say, "I just can't make the "g" into a "b"!" The student is correct as a "g" will always be a "g". What we are after here is tongue positioning. Say a "g" but LISTEN for a "b"; it is possible to say the letter "b" with the tongue positioning of the letter "g". Yes, it does take practice - if it didn't, everyone could do it and there would be nothing special about being a ventriloquist!

Some ventriloquists use a combination sound similar to trying to say a "g" and "d" at the SAME TIME. You need to press the entire surface of your tongue against the roof of your mouth and sort of "pop" the "b" sound out. This does work well but will require some sincere practice and concentration until you get the feel of it.

I strongly advise that you DO NOT use the letter "d" alone as the substitute for a "b". Why? A "d" is made with the TIP of the tongue (try it) and it is almost impossible to produce a distinct sounding "b" with the tip of the tongue alone.

Of course, you can be effective as a ventriloquist without producing totally accurate substitution sounds. There are several reasons this is true.

Saying substitution sounds out of the context of the sentence isn't always convincing but when you slip them into a sentence it works fine. Also, if you do NOT emphasize the word with the substitution sound in it but DO emphasize another important word in the sentence, this helps also. Of course, if it is the "punch" line, you will HAVE to emphasize it.

I suppose you know what is referred to in a joke as the "punch" word in the "punch line" don't you? It is the word or sentence upon which all the humor depends. Usually it is a surprise word.

To illustrate:

>F. Father asked me to do something for the family.
>V. What was it?
>F. LEAVE HOME!

"Leave home" is the punch line. It is the line that makes people laugh. In a ventriloquist dialogue, the punch words are often CAPITOLIZED.

Another example:

>V. Do you know what a caterpillar is?
>F. Sure....it's an UPHOLSTERED WORM.

In that joke (or "gag" as the jokes are sometimes called), the words "upholstered worm" are the punch words. Notice the series of "......." which indicate a slight pause in the delivery of the line just before the punch line. This pause adds to the suspense and humor of the joke. TIMING is very, very important if you are to draw from your audience it's heartiest laughter!

Now that we understand what the "punch" is (and it is extremely important to the ventriloquist) remember this: if possible, the beginner ventriloquist should avoid punch words that contain the difficult substitution sounds. It will be better for the strength of your humor. (Some might suggest that this is "cheating" which is a ridiculous suggestion. No intelligent actor would go on stage and attempt a feat of which he knew he was incapable. The ventriloquist is no different. First, do your very best with the easy words and bit-by-bit work your way into the more difficult sounds. This is not cheating; it is an act of wisdom and common sense!)

There may be some "gags" that you like so well because of their strong humor, you will want to use them in spite of the difficult sounds which they contain. There is only one way left to handle this - PRACTICE. So, let's get on with it.

Say the following sentences ventriloquially. Remember, the substitution sound for "b" is "g".

>I'd better go to the bank. The band sounds great.
>What a lovely basket of Buttercups. Beat it, Bill!
>Another beautiful "B" word and I'll be quick to burst!

Again, if you will glide over the words with the sound substitution and emphasize the other important words in the sentence, you will overcome any difference in sound.

To illustrate:

"What a lovely bouquet of roses!" In this sentence you will emphasize the word "roses" without putting too much emphasis on the word "bouquet". As you say "g̲ouquet" it won't be noticed.

Now for the last sound requiring a sound substitution, and it will be quite easy for you with the experience you've gained already.

The substitution sound for "P" is "K". Again, the important point to remember is tongue positioning. Review AGAIN the rules and reasons for sound substitution. Now for some practice:

| | | |
|---|---|---|
| Pennies | becomes | k̲ennies |
| pastry | " | k̲astry |
| pinning | " | k̲inning |
| Pauline | " | K̲auline |

Ex. 25

F. I'd like to be an artist. Painting (kainting) interests me.

V. Have you gotten started?

F. Well.....I haven't started but at least I have a paint (kaint) brush.

V. (Thoughtfully) Hmmmmmm.

F. Someone gave me a pail (kail) to use.

V. Why did they give you a pail?

F. Don't know, guess he thought I was going to paint (kaint) a HOUSE!

At first, all ventriloquial sound substitutions may seem clumsy and confusing. DON'T GET DISCOURAGED. With practice comes familiarity, and as you become familiar with the sounds they become easier to produce, and as they become easier to say you will gain CONFIDENCE. Before you know it, the sound substitutions will become a natural way of speech (ventriloquially) and require little, if any, concentration from you. Ad libs begin to slip into your act almost without warning....ventriloquism has become a FUN portion of your life....you have become a PRO!

## LESSON TEN - WHAT NOW?

Even the professional ventriloquists continue to practice daily. It is impossible to keep a skill without exercising that skill daily. Ventriloquism is a SKILL; it must be exercised to be kept.

The following exercise is to develop RESONANCE in your voice. It will relax your voice mechanism and help to improve not only your ventriloquial speech but your own natural voice as well. Use your lips FREELY on this exercise.

Ex. 26

```
mmmmm - mmmmm - mmmmm - mmmmm
mum  mum  mum  mum  mum  mum  mum
mummy    mummy    mummy    mummy
nun  nun  nun  nun  (hold it) nnnnnnnnnnnn
hum the musical scale with "n" (up and down)
hum the musical scale with "m" (up and down)
```

Ex. 27

```
HUM:
nnnnnNANnnnnnnNANnnnnnNANnnnnnNANnnnnn
nnnnnNONnnnnnnNONnnnnnNONnnnnnNONnnnnn
nnnnnNENnnnnnnNENnnnnnNENnnnnnNENnnnnn
    NGnnnnnnNGnnnnnnNGnnnnnnNGnnnnn
      nnnnnNGnnnnnnNGnnnnnnNGnnnnnNG
```

REMEMBER: the combination of the sounds of "n" and "g" naturally make the sound "ng". You, of course, had training on this in lesson eight. The throat passage is not able to retain the breath on this sound because the tongue obstructs the sound and reroutes it up and through the nose and nostrils. "M", "N", and "NG" are all made in the same manner. The "ng" sound is important to the ventriloquist and for that reason we speak of it once more in your last lesson. The reason for its importance is because right where you make the sound "ng" (up in your nose) is exactly where you must place your voice for good ventriloquial speech.

So now I want you to go back to exercise twenty-six and say it until you feel the vibration in your nose. Then touch your cheeks and you will feel the vibration there as well. Continue with the exercise until you are certain that you have your voice PLACED correctly. Then take the next test; feel to see if your breath is coming through your nose. When that is satisfactory, do this familiar exercise with our "magical" word:

shay   shay   shay   shay   shay   shay

shay   shay   shay   shay   shay   shay

Ventriloquially, this is placed exactly the same as the "ng" exercise. This is the way you can always test yourself; now, a year from now, or years from now. No matter how skilled you become as a ventriloquist, always start with THIS SAME TEST. You must be certain and KNOW you are placing your voice correctly for the art of ventriloquism. Never forget it! It is the real SECRET of true VENTRILOQUIAL VOICE.

Here is a good exercise for your tongue articulation.

    1) Do it with your VENTRIL-O-AID.
    2) Do the exercise without the VENTRIL-O-AID but do it ventriloquially.

Ex. 28

    ta ta   da da   la la   ka ka   ga ga
    ja ja   na na   ta ta   sa sa   ra ra

That may sound a little silly to you but it is wonderful as a tongue exercise. This would be a good time to stretch your tongue to a thin point five times. Okay?

Now let's do a little PANTOMIME to help you make your pal more LIFELIKE. Get him out of his suitcase and "let's pretend"!

Simply read this with him on your knee and let HIM ACT it out.

Ex. 29

V. I hear music.

F. (Looks around saying nothing. Pauses..... then looks up)

V. No, it's not UP THERE.

F. (Looks down)

V. No, it's not downstairs.

F. (Looks under the chair)

V. No, it isn't there either; in fact, it seems far away.

F. (Looks out the window or through a doorway. The ventriloquist should not move. The figure does all the acting)

V. It's pretty music.

F. (Looks at you and then sways his shoulders and his entire body)

V. (You take a paper from the table and start reading to yourself)

F. (Leans over - looks at paper - starts to read it also)

V. (You catch him at it)

F. (Looks up at you)

V. (You scold him)

F. (Hangs head)

V. (You laugh)

F. (Looks relieved)

- END -

Have you ever heard the siren of a fire engine, ambulance, or police car coming down the street? It was a shrill, loud sound, yet you could not tell from which direction it was coming. The ear can hear a sound but we often depend upon our eyes to determine the direction from which the sound comes. This fact makes ventriloquism possible.

Therefore, isn't it reasonable that if you speak for a little fellow whose mouth is only a FEW INCHES from yours, and do so with good lip control in a voice that is different than your own, that your audience will not be able to distinguish between his mouth and yours as to where the voice is coming? So, have PLENTY of confidence in yourself and your pal. Put wit and humor into his mouth and have FUN TOGETHER.

HERE'S WISHING YOU MUCH SUCCESS!

FOR YOUR FURTHER STUDY

VENTRILOQUISM FROM A-V by Bill Andersen. If it concerns ventriloquism, it's probably discussed in this book. A wide variety of information arranged alphabetically by subject. A great help to any aspiring ventriloquist.

VENTRILOQUISM FOR CHILDREN AND ADULTS. This excellent 40 minute training VIDEO lets you watch as you laugh and learn. Step by step demonstration by school show specialist, Steve Chaney.

DEVELOPING CHARACTER VOICES. A wonderful audio cassette tape prepared by voice specialist, Liz Von Seggen. Over 15 different voices taught on this single cassette.

WRITE YOUR OWN SCRIPTS by Bill Andersen, one of the most popular writers of ventriloquist material. Learn the various types of routines and how to put each one together, from beginning to end.

MAKE YOUR OWN DUMMY. The only book of its kind! This is a complete set of plans for building a professional ventriloquist figure. Complete with illustrations and photos.

For more information on these and other ventriloquist materials, see your dealer or write the publisher of this book.